D0249542

"A man went down to Panama
Where many a man had died ...
A man stood up in Panama
And the mountains stood aside."

Percy MacKaye, 1913

The Story of Vernon C. Luthas, M.D.

Loma Linda University School of Medicine

(formerly College of Medical Evangelists)

Class of 1953-B

By Ruthie Jacobsen

2011

And the Mountains Stood Aside

Ruthie Jacobsen, author

Don Jacobsen, editor

Cover and interior design, Diane Baier, D.Zyne Co.

Published by HighWalk Productions, Inc.
P.O. Box 26, Hiawassee, GA 30546

ISBN: 978-1-4507-7698-1

Printed in U.S.A.

"And the Mountains Stood Aside" is available at Christian bookstores and Amazon.com. To order direct or for quantity pricing go to: bookorder@luthasbook.com.

"I say unto you, if you have faith … like a grain of mustard seed, you can say to this mountain, 'Move from here to yonder place,' and it will move, and nothing will be impossible to you."

Matthew 17:21, Amplified Bible

"Before the intrepid spirit and unwavering faith of a Zerubbabel (or a Dr. Vernon Luthas), great mountains of difficulty will become a plain."

Prophets and Kings, p. 595

Lovingly dedicated to
Diane and David Doucette,
rays of sunshine to any parent's heart ...

Table of Contents

	Introduction	*xiii*
one	*Dusty, Shaken, But Unbroken*	1
two	*Foothills*	13
three	*God and Some of His Friends*	25
four	*A Mountain? Stamp it "Moved"*	35
five	*Expensive Expansions*	45
six	*No Wonder They Call it Amazing*	55
seven	*Kettering's Own Brother Benjamin*	67
eight	*Did You Know?*	75
nine	*His Friends Said ...*	81
ten	*Epilogue*	89

Introduction

On the hot, humid Thursday morning of July 2, 1863, Colonel Joshua Chamberlain of the Union Army was given staggering orders. This was an initial skirmish of the battle of Little Round Top near Gettysburg—the battle in which more Americans would die than any other in her history. As the well-equipped Southern troops advanced up the hill, Chamberlain was told to hold the left edge of the line at all costs.

The Union Army had been languishing against the South and this would be a decisive battle. Time and again on that Thursday Confederate soldiers charged up the hill. Time and again Chamberlain and his ragged troops, now dangerously low on ammunition, turned them back.

Near noon, after repelling the South's fourth charge, only 80 of Chamberlain's original 300 men remained alive. Ammunition? Perhaps a handful of bullets each. Undaunted, and driven by the force of the order he had been given, Colonel Chamberlain jumped to his feet waving his sword over his head, shouting the order to fix bayonets—and charge! He told his men, "Retreat is not an option. I may be killed, but it will not be with a bullet in my back!"

Stunned by this display of raw courage, the Confederate soldiers were thrown into a panic and laid down their weapons. History would define this victory as a moment of destiny for the nation. Historians would say that if the South had won our continent would likely have looked very much like Europe, a mosaic of loosely-linked countries. There probably would not have been a United States of America—one nation under God, indivisible—strong enough, for instance during the Second World War, to fight major wars in two hemispheres and win them both.

"When God places His hand on a life, the results are dramatic."

Joshua L. Chamberlain was a schoolteacher from Maine. He had become an instant colonel in the Union Army, not because he was a skilled warrior, but because he was the first man in Maine to show up and volunteer. Later, Chamberlain, writing of the battle, would say that he sensed the "Hand of Providence" directing the affairs of the struggling, infant nation. He was a man of deep faith and sensed that his was a nation of destiny in the plan of God.

Colonel Chamberlain was driven by a dream, a dream of a United States, a land of freedom for all, a land of peace and justice. That dream shaped every decision he made and gave purpose to his making it.

As significant as were the battles around Gettysburg in 1863, there is an even greater battle, a more significant war, raging in our world. It is the war between right and wrong, between darkness and light, between good and evil. In that war, too, the "Hand of

Providence" is searching for unpretentious, common, ordinary men and women who are driven by His dream, and through whom He can change His world. Through them God still shows Himself strong, still today, as the Mountain-Mover.

This book is about such a man: Vernon C. Luthas, MD.

It is my privilege to know him. It will be your privilege too.

When God places His hand on a life, the results are dramatic. He can move mountains as He works through His children, and for reasons of His own He has always found ordinary people:

A sheepherder who said his tongue got tangled; he was sure he could never speak before Pharaoh, or a crowd of Israelites. But Moses became God's great person-in-charge to free an entire nation.

A lovely young woman who had learned early in life to trust a big God, and He used Esther to rescue His people from a savage obliteration.

A teenager with a slingshot and a few smooth rocks who ran to a giant mountain of a man in the name of the God of Israel, and David saw that mountain crumble at his feet.

An unpretentious Spanish-speaking Chinese lad from Panama who came to the United States penniless but with a dream in his heart, and who spent his life watching mountains "stand aside."

We look back on dramatic events in Scripture and what was accomplished through God's ordinary people then, and we want to call the men and women heroes—champions, but no doubt each of them would assure us that they were frail in their own eyes and totally dependent on a God they knew was Almighty. They were brave because they knew He was strong.

Caleb, even at an advanced age, was fearless and ready to tackle the mountain country filled with giants because all his life he had had opportunities to practice his faith. He had seen his God move mountains of difficulty. His God had assured him, over and over, “Do not be afraid,” and Caleb had learned to take God at His word. Caleb was ordinary; his God was not. Vernon Luthas is ordinary; his God is not.

We are stunned by the unique ways God worked—who would have expected high stone walls to collapse just because some folks walked around the city? They had no weapons, but they had the ark of God, His circumstance-changing, promise-fulfilling presence.

Who would have guessed that a huge sea would part, exposing an ocean bed as dry as a sidewalk—just because a man held a stick out over the water?

Who knew that three young men would calmly walk out of a white-hot brick kiln unharmed and without even smelling like smoke?

The people we see as grand examples—the Joshuas, the Davids, the Josephs—had more than earthly success, giftedness or perseverance. These were people whose lives were clearly directed by God and they knew it. And they watched mountains stand aside.

God is still moving mountains today.

As you walk with Vernon Luthas through the pages of this book your faith will be fortified to realize again how God works in any life where He is invited.

Vernon was born in Panama. Ever wished to visit there? You’re about to. Read on.

– Chapter 1 –

Dusty, Shaken, But Unbroken

If you have ever visited there, you know why the Panama Canal is ranked as one of the engineering wonders of the modern world. Prior to its construction the only route from the Pacific to the Atlantic Ocean was to travel the 7,872 miles around Cape Horn at the southern tip of South America. But it is less than 50 miles from one end of the Panama Canal to the other; time of passage—about eight hours!

Discussions about building a canal to join the oceans had gone on among the seafaring nations of the world for centuries, but the actual construction proved to be an unprecedented nightmare. Begun by the French in 1880 with Ferdinand De Lesseps, builder of the Suez Canal as chief organizer, the project was doomed from the beginning. Even the finest French engineering could not design around the clouds of omnipresent mosquitoes that rose from the swamps.

Finally, after nearly two decades, the French decided that the cost was too high and pulled out, leaving the "big ditch" largely unfinished. They left behind nearly 22,000 graves of French workers and their families who had died from accident, yellow fever, typhoid, and malaria. The aborted, ill-fated project was sold to the United States.

The Americans quickly learned that they hadn't bought a bargain. At times the task seemed impossible, the forests impenetrable, the mountains immovable, the mosquitoes unconquerable. The engineering feat alone was without precedent in the history of the world; the human toll was even greater. Six thousand American graves would soon dot the landscape, but President Theodore Roosevelt's determination to join the world's two great oceans kept the project inching forward.

Army doctor William Gorgas knew that the only way to alleviate the health problems was to destroy the mosquitoes that carried the diseases. He ordered homes, hospitals, and work stations to be fumigated. Swamps and marshes were drained and roads paved. Despair slowly turned to hope. Before the canal was completed the project would employ more than 250,000 people from all over the world.

The first ship passed through the completed canal on September 26, 1913—a third of a century after it was begun. It was a landmark event in the history of the world.

Among those who ventured from their homes to help in the completion of the project were workers from China. Vernon Luthas' grandparents were among them. Recruiters were sent from Panama and assured the Chinese that signing on to the project was their ticket to the promised land ... a promise, they would all soon learn, that was not easily kept.

Vernon's grandfather, whose sir name was Chin, was called Luthau, which meant "elder brother," by the men he supervised on the job. He was a good foreman, kind, diligent, and fair. The name stuck and was later anglicized to Luthas because of political turmoil in the country. Luthau, the favored foreman, met a girl from China, who had also immigrated to Panama; they were married and made Panama their home.

Their son, Vernon's father, Edward Lim Chin grew up with the sights and sounds of the giant construction project daily ringing in his ears. He would marry his sweetheart, Claudia, and it was here, in their adopted country, that Vernon, his brother Carlton, and their younger sister Irma, were born. Life wasn't perfect and was far from easy, but they felt the security of a loving home; parents and grandparents doted on the children.

Vernon's mother became a Christian and took her children to Sunday School on occasion. Later she was invited to study the Bible with some friends and became a member of the Seventh-day Adventist Church. This new relationship with her God became her focus and her hope, and it became her heart's desire for her children to follow her in her beliefs.

"Vernon's mother became a Christian ... this new relationship with her God became her focus and hope."

Vernon's father was never very impressed with the "poor little Adventist church" in their city. He attended once or twice and was uncomfortable to see his friends and family actually washing each other's feet![1] It irritated dad Luthas to see that this little group was

[1] Foot washing, accompanied by the more familiar Communion Service, is a biblical teaching observed in Seventh-day Adventist congregations, generally four times each year.

happy in such simple and crude surroundings. It didn't compare with the other ornate churches he saw in Panama City, the capitol, where they lived. What he couldn't yet see was that they were there to meet with their big God—who doesn't look at outward appearances, but at the heart.

Vernon's father had only a third grade education, but he wanted his three children to be able to go to school and learn everything he had missed. He became a professional gambler, racing horses, and later, greyhounds. His horses were quite profitable, but when his business got, as he would later say, "too crooked," he started racing dogs. As a child, Vernon loved animals and remembers the exciting sights and sounds of the races.

"A father of the fatherless, ... and a protector ... is God." Psalm 68:6

Even though Dad Luthas decided his wife's religion was not for him, he never opposed her in her beliefs. The children always went to church with her because what Mama Luthas said was law. As a 10-year-old, Vernon wasn't always excited about attending the little church; he could see his father's reluctance, but he went because his mother insisted. Carlton and Irma accompanied them and there in that humble little place seeds were planted in his heart that would later sprout with new vitality.

Since the birth of the Seventh-day Adventist Church in the mid-nineteenth century, there has always been a strongly-held commitment to share the truths of God's Word all around the world, and to this humble little church, in the small country of

Panama, a family of enthusiastic believers, the Dunns, had come from America as missionaries. They would soon become trusted friends of the Luthas family.

One day when Vernon was 12 and Carlton 13, the Dunns came to the Luthas parents with a plan. They were leaving soon for the United States on furlough, and urged that the boys should go there, too. They promised to help them get enrolled in a Christian school—which was not available in Panama at the time. They were certain that the boys could find work to cover their tuition and other expenses.

"But how would I ever pay, even for the trip?" their reluctant father asked. "Borrow the money," the missionaries urged, "and God will provide." So Dad Luthas borrowed $500 and sent the two brothers to the "land of opportunity"—on a banana boat.

Frightened and feeling very much alone, the two set out on an unknown adventure. They had never been away from home, and now they were leaving for a foreign country. For how long? No one knew.

But they were not alone. Angels were watching over her precious children because a loving mother arose every morning at 2:00 AM and prayed for her sons. That was her sacred hour with God. She no longer had direct influence over them, but she would still cover them with the power of her prayers. She relied on the promises of God's word, like this one:

"A father of the fatherless, ... and a protector ... is God."
Psalm 68:6

The boys were treated kindly on the boat. They ate their meals at the Captain's table (there were only 12 passengers and crew). At each stop in the Central American countries, a fresh load of bananas was brought on board. After five long but exciting days their boat ride was over and they pulled into the harbor at New Orleans, Louisiana.

However, a new and unexpected drama was about to unfold. They were met by an unsympathetic Customs officer who explained that because they were not bonded and had no security, they must return to Panama and could not even leave the boat!

Vernon and Carlton walked to the far end of the ship behind a pile of freight where they knelt and Vernon prayed his first real prayer. He cried as he told God their troubles and asked for a miracle. They didn't have the money needed for the bond and no return ticket home. They could see no way out of their dilemma.

The officials contacted Dad Luthas and he was quickly able to borrow another $500 for each of them. The funds were held by the Immigration officials in Panama in the event that the under-age boys had to return home for any reason. (Later, when they received student visas, the $1,000 was returned to their father.) By nightfall the boys were given the good news; thankful and relieved, they were allowed to enter the United States! It was a door they sensed God was supernaturally opening.

Once on shore they looked for someone to help them. The Dunns were not able to be there until the next day, but again, God provided—He was hearing a mother's petitions. Now they were met by another Customs officer, but this man was much more approachable than the first. He questioned them and asked what they needed. When he heard their story he told them he had two boys about their ages, so if they wished he would take them home for the night. Ahhh, a bath, a warm meal, a bed, and a safe place until their friends, the Dunns, were able to meet them the next morning and take them to their new home.

Traveling by train from New Orleans to Keene, Texas, they were seeing new country, new sights. They sensed God was keeping His hand on them because they knew their mother was keeping her daily appointment with God.

"They sensed God was keeping His hand on them because they knew their mother was keeping her daily appointment with God."

When the boys arrived on the campus of what would later become Southwestern Adventist University, they were taken in as part of the campus family. In fact, they soon became favorites. Carlton enrolled in the academy (high school), and Vernon was in the 8th grade.

They were the only Oriental students on campus that year, and though they were young they were always treated with kindness and respect. Vernon and Carlton, true to their agreement, began immediately "working their way." They were soon to discover that people on campus not only welcomed them, but were eager to help.

The boys' first job was mowing lawns, and for their hard work in the hot Texas sun, they were paid a whopping 18¢/hr. But soon young Vernon, at 12 already the budding entrepreneur, devised a plan. He learned a new word and decided that in addition to yard work, he would need to "moonlight." His motivation was to replace his one pair of high-mileage shoes. So he bought a small can of shoe polish and went door-to-door in the men's dormitory every Friday afternoon, shining shoes for 10¢ a pair. If he could do three pairs of shoes in an hour, he found that he could about double his lawn-mowing salary.

They were happy, hard-working, and likeable young kids who were tending to business, and determined to make their way in this new country. Like Joseph in the Bible story, God blessed everything they did because of their faithfulness and the prayers of their mother.

"Dr. Harry Hamilton, President of the College, was so impressed with these two youngsters on his campus that he wrote a letter to their parents."

Even Dr. Harry Hamilton, President of the College, was so impressed with these two youngsters on his campus that he wrote a letter to their parents. "Your boys are an example to everyone here." he told their parents. "They are industrious, honest, happy lads and we're glad to have them." Mother Luthas breathed a sigh and a prayer of gratitude. The significance of Dr. Hamilton's letter was not lost on Dad Luthas, either.

The environment wasn't perfect. Eighth-graders generally have no trouble finding mischief, but even in some of the "sideline opportunities" that could have pulled him in the wrong direction, God had a protective shield around Vernon. There were doubtless two reasons—their mother was praying, and they were kept busy—study/work, study/work—long days, short nights.

In a new school system with a totally new curriculum, Vernon soon found that he was behind the others in his studies. His teacher, Miss Moyer, was sensitive to his situation and took extra time with him. With her gentle, kindhearted tutoring, in a matter of weeks he had caught up with his class. Here he saw another Christian in action, and it had an impact on him. She took him under her wing and he thrived. He was bright and motivated; he needed only a little time and a little encouragement.

At 12 and 13 he and Carlton were baptized in the church on campus. Vernon will tell you that much of the credit for that decision goes to his dear friend Miss Moyer. Years later, as a successful physician, Vernon would go back to Keene, Texas, walk into her office, and give his tutor and friend the hug of gratitude they both knew she richly deserved.

When Vern was in the 9th grade, tragedy struck back home. Dad Luthas had become gravely ill. As his condition worsened, the family didn't know where to turn for help. His wife was quietly praying for wisdom and once more the American missionaries appeared with the answer. The Dunns described the good medical care available at Loma Linda Hospital in California, and Mom and Dad Luthas were again able to borrow the money, fly to Los Angeles, and from there make their way to Loma Linda.

Dr. Alton Butterfield, a surgeon and Chief of the Medical Staff, examined the senior Luthas and discovered that he had advanced tuberculosis, severe untreated diabetes, and by any measure was critically ill. Dr. Butterfield gathered a group of his trusted medical colleagues and nurses around his patient's bed and prayed for God's healing.

As Ed Luthas lay in his bed listening to their prayers for him, he was surprised by this kind of tender care. Their faith in a big God was real. Here was a man they hardly knew but they were pleading with the God of the universe to intervene and save his life. He never forgot their genuine care for a very ill man from a far country.

The next morning Dad Luthas awoke with a sense that God had already begun a work of healing in his body. Two weeks later all the symptoms of tuberculosis were gone and the diabetes was under control. He had come to the hospital debilitated and without hope, but he walked out a new man. Everyone who had seen the "before and after" knew they had witnessed a miracle.

The morning of his discharge from the hospital, the Luthases were told that they must stay close by for further medical care, so they began to lay plans to make Loma Linda their home. This meant that they could be closer to their boys. Before the day was over, Mother Luthas was on the phone attempting to reach the boys in Texas. How would they feel about making America their new home and reuniting the family in California?

Consensus was easy; the vote was four to zero! (Irma would come from Panama later.) Mother Luthas wired funds to Keene, Texas, and two days later the boys were on the train from Dallas, headed for Southern California.

The train trip itself proved to be memorable. This was 1942 and America was at war. Young Vernon and Carlton would soon discover that they were the only passengers on the train who were not American soldiers. Once the GIs discovered they had youngsters on board, the boys were instant "junior civilian celebrities" and they basked in the attention.

Another interesting wrinkle developed; although their tickets were written to Loma Linda, California, they discovered that the train depot had not yet been built in Loma Linda. Hmm. The Conductor came up with a daring solution. As they approached Loma Linda, the engineer slowed the train to a crawl. The boys, standing on the platform between the cars, tossed their suitcases, and then, with a hundred GIs cheering, they jumped!

They had arrived—dusty, shaken, but unbroken ... ready for a happy reunion with Mom and Dad after a two-year separation.

"They had arrived—dusty, shaken, but unbroken ... ready for a happy reunion with Mom and Dad after a two-year separation."

Two nurses from the hospital, and later a pastor, visited the Luthases and sensed a spiritual hunger in Dad Luthas' heart. They invited themselves to the Luthas apartment to answer his questions about the Bible. He was seeing a bigger God than he had found in Panama City. God was healing not only his body, but his soul. A few months later there was a golden moment and a long-awaited baptism at the Loma Linda Hill Seventh-day Adventist Church. The Luthas family was now together, healthy, and redeemed— forever changed.

Long journey, but God had moved the mountains necessary to get them where He wanted them to be.

– Chapter 2 –

Foothills

Vernon and Carlton were enrolled by their parents for their high school years at La Sierra Academy near Riverside, not far from Loma Linda.

While in Loma Linda, Vernon met two Chinese medical students who took an interest in him and instilled a great desire in him to be a physician. They were his heroes. One of the students, Frances Lau, would become a cardiologist; the other, Alfred Liu, would become a thoracic surgeon. Both would later teach at the School of Medicine at Loma Linda University. Meanwhile they had become Vernon's inspiration.

After completing his high school years Vernon packed his bags and enrolled as a freshman at Pacific Union College (PUC) in northern California. Now he had a goal—now he had a dream. He would study hard, make the best grades possible, and he would apply as a medical student at the College of Medical Evangelists in Loma Linda.

Four years later when he made application to the School of Medicine at Loma Linda, the Pacific Union College faculty also sent their recommendation—but it wasn't just a good reference for a good student. He was their number one choice. It was the highest commendation a faculty could give.

Weeks of anxious waiting later the response came from the medical school. Vernon rushed to his dorm room for some solitude as he tore into the envelope to discover what he knew was going to be the most important news of his life and the opening of a huge new door into his future. The words blurred on the page as he read that his application had been denied!

Vern was crushed. He had done his best but now the doors were closed. His faculty advisor was dumfounded. In desperation, Vern walked, he wept, and he talked to God. He finally found himself on Old Winery Road not far from campus, wrestling with God and in despair. As he fell on his knees on the old dirt road he came to the end of himself; God spoke to him there. Vernon will tell you, "That's where I had a major heart change. God changed my life on that dirt road that day."

As he listened, the Lord seemed to say to him, "Vernon, I know you've worked hard, but all your success has not been because of anything you did. Rather it is because I have blessed you and kept My hand on your life. Your success in the future will all depend on your relationship to Me. Can you trust Me with that?"

"Don't be afraid. I have redeemed you … you are mine! When you walk through deep waters, I will be with you." Isaiah 42:16, 17

As he walked back to his room on campus the sky seemed bluer, the PUC mountains not as steep. He could hold his head high because he was a different person. God had met him and he knew his life was not his own.

A few days later Vern was offered a job as a carpenter's apprentice for the summer, building barns. The future was uncertain but somehow he was at peace. Two weeks before the Loma Linda Medical School term was to begin, the second letter came. The Admissions Committee notified him that one spot had become available (because of the tragic death of another applicant) and Vernon had been accepted! Vernon C. Luthas would be a doctor! The idea was almost too immense for him to comprehend.

Money was tight, but again and again God demonstrated that He was sufficient for those kinds of mountains, too. While at La Sierra Academy Vernon had made some wonderful friends. Among them were Dr. Henry Barron and his wife, whom everyone called Mama Barron. After Vern arrived back in the Loma Linda area, the Barrons invited he and his brother to their home to give them a hand. There Vern learned to bale hay, to milk cows, to build fences, and to shovel ... well, whatever needed to be shoveled.

"Don't be afraid. I have redeemed you ... you are mine! When you walk through deep waters, I will be with you." Isaiah 42:16, 17

Mrs. Barron paid the $200 for his first entrance fee to medical school, and he was off and running. During the summers, he sold Christian books door-to-door. Later he worked as an extern at the Glendale Sanitarium between school terms.

While he had been a student at PUC Vernon had joined the Hawaiian Club where he had met a pretty pre-nursing student named Betty Kim. Even when they weren't together he found himself spending a lot of time thinking about her. It sure made his life a lot more interesting.

Betty was a challenge because she was busy, and besides she was dating a student at the University of Southern California. But one day Vern smiled his handsomest smile and convinced her to go out to dinner with him. Well, actually, he was taking her to a free meal at his cousin's house because that fit his budget better.

As they stood at his cousin's front door, Vernon rang the doorbell, but the noise in the house must have covered the sound because no one answered. As they waited on the porch, he looked at Betty and thought, "I love this girl!" and quickly kissed her. It took them both by surprise; it was their first date, but it would be the first of many.

"... And beyond the dim unknown, standeth GOD among the shadows, keeping watch above His own."

J.G. Whittier

Betty would later tell her friends that she "dumped" her friend at USC for a penniless medical student. After she finished her nursing degree, they were married; by this time Vern was a sophomore medical student. He said he waited to marry her till she finished school so she could support him. She said she had waited to see if he was going to make it through his first year of med school. So began a life-long eventful journey together.

How does God place His people exactly where He wants them, and at the precise time He will need them there to do something for His kingdom? Ask Joseph, or ask Nehemiah how God orchestrated the events for them. Ask Esther and Daniel how God daily used them in a specific place to shape events for His purposes.

John Greenleaf Whittier, the Quaker poet who died in 1892, got it right, when he said, "… And beyond the dim unknown, standeth GOD among the shadows, keeping watch above His own."

God was "keeping watch" in Vernon's life, and just as God moved in the lives of His children in Scripture He still works today. He doesn't answer prayer in the same way twice. Maybe that's because if we knew exactly how He would work, we would look to the answer or event, instead of asking only for His sovereign will. He wants our hearts and an ever-deepening relationship of trust and dependence.

When Vernon graduated from medical school—then known as the College of Medical Evangelists—and after a year of internship and a year of surgery residency, he was inducted into the US Navy. Because the 11 other fledgling physicians who were inducted with him were immediately sent overseas, Vernon assumed that he would be also. The long weeks of anticipated separation from Betty caused a pall of gloom to settle over both of them.

When he inquired about the Navy's plans for him, Vern and Betty were surprised to discover that he had not been issued any orders at all. The Admiral couldn't understand it, either. He finally checked with the Department of the Navy in Washington DC, and was told it had been decided to station Vern at the Naval Hospital in Corona, California, which was within driving distance of Loma Linda. They didn't even have to move, they could stay in their home while Vern served his country at the nearby Navy Hospital.

Vernon asked for Sabbath privileges, and was told that he would be "watched" first, to see if he could be trusted. Some had used these privileges carelessly, and the officers over Vernon wanted to see if he was for real. They soon were happy to discover that he was.

Early in his medical career, Vernon began praying with his patients because he knew that God could touch them in deeper ways and for all kinds of healing. The young doctor wanted more than anything to speak a word of encouragement, to share hope where it was needed. A corpsman, Richard McDowell, recently assigned to Vern, was intrigued as he saw the consistent life of this humble Christian man who only wanted to do his best for his God and for his patients. As they made rounds, Dr. Vernon didn't realize how carefully he was being scrutinized. Corpsman McDowell was learning much about good medical techniques from his doctor friend.

He liked the way Dr. Luthas interacted with his patients, how he made treatment decisions. But most of all Richard was surprised to discover that Dr. Vernon saw his role as assistant to the Great Physician. His unselfish influence and genuine caring in the hospital were appreciated by these GIs he served, many of whom had been traumatized by war.

Richard was intrigued to observe that Dr. Luthas prayed with his patients. This was a totally new experience for the corpsman. He had never seen anything just like it before. Here was a highly trained and knowledgeable physician who was truly depending on help from God.

Before long, Richard was asking questions, all kinds of questions that could only be answered by digging together into God's word. It became a weekly ritual—they met together every Friday night. But before he could get all of his questions answered, in true military fashion, Richard was re-assigned and sent to another post of duty. Vernon gave him some things to study and helped him enroll in a Bible correspondence course, but the two men would lose contact. Dr. Vernon would wonder, "Did Richard ever accept Christ as his Lord and Savior? Was his life really changed?

More than five years would pass before Vernon would have the answer to his questions. Yes, in fact, Richard had given his heart to Christ, had been baptized, and had just been accepted for medical school at the College of Medical Evangelists. He told Vernon that his goal was to become "just like you." Vernon thanked God for being a part of the influence God used to bring Richard to faith in Christ and a life of service.

"Vernon began praying with his patients because he knew that God could touch them in deeper ways and for all kinds of healing."

Do you believe that God chooses us for our roles in life? Do you believe that He can and will use anyone whose life is surrendered to Him? What a future-altering insight, that God has a specific purpose for your life. His plans and purposes for you are always greater than you would ever choose or could even imagine. Someone has observed that the two most important days in a person's life are the day he is born and the day he discovers why.

Gideon didn't even want to be a leader. Neither did Joshua, Moses, Esther, or Joshua Chamberlain. Dr. Luthas didn't have that as his goal either. These all realized that they were simply able to fulfill the assignment because they were following His instructions.

He promises that when we know Him intimately,

"He will make [us] strong and able to do bold and daring things for His glory." Daniel 11:32 RSV

"... But the people who know their God shall be strong and carry out great exploits." Daniel 11:32b NKJV

But we shouldn't get ahead of the story. ... Vernon's time in the Navy was going pretty well. He and Betty had settled in, had begun to work on paying down those pesky school bills, and were even discussing starting a family. About halfway through his two years of military service, without warning the Corona Naval Hospital was closed and Vernon was reassigned. The song he and Betty found themselves singing sounded like, "Here we come, Beaufort Naval Hospital, Beaufort, South Carolina!"

As Vernon and his family traveled eastward, they stopped in Ohio to visit a classmate from medical school, Dr. George Harding, whose grandfather had established a Mental Health facility in Worthington, near the state capitol of Columbus.

When Dr. Harding learned of Vernon's interest in an Anesthesia residency, he wanted to introduce him to his uncle, Andy Wooley, who was in an anesthesia residency program at that time at Ohio State University. The Chief of Anesthesia there was world-renowned Dr. Jay Jacoby. The name Jacoby rang a bell for Vernon. Before leaving Southern California, a close friend had said casually to Vernon, "Dr. Jay Jacoby is the best there is. He is Chair of the Department at Ohio State University and you will not find a better program anywhere."

The Luthases had planned to return to California where they had family and friends after his term of service with the Navy was completed, but they were finding something very appealing about this discussion in Ohio. "Would you like to meet Dr. Jacoby?" Andy asked him. "Would I!" Vern replied. So Andy took Vernon to his friend, Dr. Jay Jacoby.

"Are you a Seventh-day Adventist—like Andy?" Dr. Jacoby asked. "Yes, I am," Vernon answered, wondering about the implications of the question. He soon discovered that Andy was a respected resident, and had become one of Dr. Jacoby's most highly trusted students.

"He will make [us] strong and able to do bold and daring things for His glory."

Daniel 11:32 RSV

So Dr. Jacoby invited Vernon to come to Ohio State University for his Anesthesia residency. But there were these mountains in the way. First, Vernon had already applied and been accepted for an Anesthesia residency at his alma mater in Loma Linda. Second, the Ohio State University residency had an opening in July, but Vernon didn't finish his Navy tour until the following December. Ohio State only accepted new residents in July.

As they talked, Dr. Jacoby made it clear that because of Andy's influence, he very much wanted Vernon in his program.

God was obviously about to move a mountain. "Never mind about that," Dr. Jacoby said. "It's true, we only take new residents in July. But I will save a place for you, and you can enter the program in December." So, that mountain stood aside. Vernon walked out of the Ohio State University Hospital that morning, into a brighter sunlight, with a new assurance of God's intimacy. Vernon will tell you that the words of Isaiah were very true for him that morning:

"... Before they call, I will answer, and while they are still speaking, I will hear." Isaiah 65:24 NKJV

"... Before they call, I will answer, and while they are still speaking, I will hear." Isaiah 65:24 NKJV

Once again God showed His presence, and that He does have a plan and purpose for His children.

"For I know the thoughts that I think toward you, says the Lord ... to give you a future and a hope. Then you will call upon Me, and go and pray to Me, and I will listen to you. And you will seek Me and find Me, when you search for Me with all your heart." Jeremiah 29: 11-13 NKJV

And God had another surprise for Vern. His friend, Dean Johnson, a classmate and basketball buddy from Loma Linda, joined the Ohio State University Anesthesia residency program one year later. That was a big bonus for Vernon, and for Dean, because they became a trusted duo and became known for the exceptional quality of their work.

Many people who know both Drs. Luthas and Johnson will tell you that they have much in common—they have a great work ethic and a commitment to excellence. But they brought to the operating room, along with their expertise and skill, a sweet and humble spirit. God held first place in their lives, and they were soon known, as Joseph and Joshua were known, for their integrity. They were also known for "going the second mile." They were obviously in earnest about medicine as ministry.

The course of the entire journey was not clear, but it was obvious they had at least a better view of the lay of the land from here in the foothills.

"God resists the proud, but gives grace to the humble. Therefore, humble yourselves under the mighty hand of God, that He may exalt you in due time." 1 Peter 5:5, 6 NKJV

– Chapter 3 –

God and Some of His Friends

Late one afternoon as Vernon was nearing the conclusion of his Anesthesia Residency at Ohio State University, he received one of those defining phone calls. It was from Harley Rice, Director of the world-wide medical ministry of the Seventh-day Adventist Church. Dr. Rice had an urgent request. "Dr. Vernon," he began, "Eugene Kettering is planning to build a beautiful new hospital in Kettering, Ohio, a southern suburb of Dayton, to be owned and managed by the Seventh-day Adventist Church. It is scheduled to be finished in 1964. Vernon," he said, "we need the best Anesthesia Department available. Can you come and help us?"

What an honor! What a challenge! He and Betty had never even discussed remaining in Ohio. They were looking eagerly westward to California where their family and friends were anticipating their return. But they prayed. And they listened. Finally, Vernon told his wife, "Betty, we have told the Lord that we wanted to go to the mission field, and serve in a mission hospital. Maybe He is saying that Ohio is our mission field." Betty agreed. They prayed again and had instant peace with their decision.

Several days later they drove to Kettering to meet with George

Nelson, the man who would be president of the Kettering Hospital, Paul Reichert, treasurer-elect, and others. They saw the plans and were captured by the dream of what Kettering Hospital could become. The visit confirmed their decision that this was indeed to be their mission field.

But God had an even more dramatic plan to confirm the Luthas' call to Kettering. A few days after their decision had been made, the phone rang again. It was Dr. George Bruggerman, head of Anesthesiology at Miami Valley Hospital in Dayton, inviting Vernon to serve on their anesthesiology staff. The Kettering Hospital wouldn't be completed for several years, but God wanted Vernon in Dayton now to establish his practice and his presence there during the intervening time. Having taken his residency at Ohio State University, Vernon already had his Ohio medical license, so again, on God's timetable, He put Vernon in Dayton, exactly when He wanted him there.

So it was that in 1960, the Luthas family moved to Kettering, only 100 miles west of Columbus where he had just finished his residency. Vernon worked there for the next three years with the Dayton Anesthesia Group, serving Miami Valley and Good Samaritan Hospitals under the direction of Dr. Jay Stahler, a prominent anesthesiologist. It was invaluable experience for a young, fledgling physician.

Just one week after beginning his duties in Dayton, Dr. Vernon was summoned to an operating room where a patient had become seriously destabilized during surgery for a brain tumor. As he entered the OR, the gravity of the situation hit him. All he could see of the patient was the top of her head. The surgeons had stopped the procedure and stepped aside. They needed help, and had called Vernon. He could get no pulse, no respiration, no blood pressure.

Instinctively Vernon began praying out loud there in the OR. He said, "Lord, I can't do this, but You can ... You are the Great Physician. Please give us wisdom to know what to do." And he went to work expecting God's wisdom; God rewards faith. Within fifteen minutes the patient was stabilized with a strong, steady pulse, normal respiration, and normal blood pressure. Vern told the surgeons, "Go ahead, you can finish your surgery. She'll be fine." Everyone in the room that day sensed that they had witnessed an event they would not soon forget.

"You are the Great Physician. Please give us wisdom to know what to do."

It became a common reality that Vern's patients seemed to have less fear and more peace as they faced surgery because he had prayed with them. He became the anesthesiologist of choice. Physicians and staff whose family members might be facing surgery would request Dr. Vernon to serve as their anesthesiologist. Word soon spread through the several hospitals where Vernon practiced, that here was a "praying doctor" and he was overwhelmed as God opened more and more ministry doors.

After Vernon had been with the Dayton group for only a year, he was approached by the chief of anesthesia. "We need another anesthesiologist," he was told, "and we want someone just like you."

Dr. Dean Johnson was just finishing his residency, also at Ohio State, and when Dean joined the group the physicians and other hospital staff became aware that their anesthesiology department had just received a strong, new, praying team member.

A year later Vernon received the same request again, "We need another outstanding anesthesiologist; could you find another one just like you and Dean?" Dr. Louis Turner, who had been teaching Anesthesia at the University of Pennsylvania, was recruited by Vernon, and stepped in. Now there were three Seventh-day Adventist anesthesiologists in the group.

Only Thomas Edison owned more patents than "Boss Ket."

Their anesthesia group was soon recognized as the best in Dayton, and when Kettering Hospital opened in 1964, (by now there were five Seventh-day Adventists in the group), all five came to the Anesthesiology Department of the new hospital. With this caliber of support specialists at Kettering Hospital, the best surgeons in the area were drawn to practice there. They knew they had been working with the best and didn't want to lose that advantage. The anesthesia group soon "raised the bar" with their creative new afternoon surgery schedules, epidurals for obstetrics, and the quality and caring demonstrated by all in the group.

At this point in the story it is not uncommon to ask, How did it happen that the Seventh-day Adventist Church ended up owning and operating a magnificent new 300-bed tertiary hospital—as a gift? Thereby hangs a story of the providence of God and the generosity of some of His friends.

Enter Charles Franklin Kettering—outstanding mind, amazing talents, uncommon gifts. Only Thomas Edison owned more patents than "Boss Ket."

Mr. Kettering grew up in Dayton and graduated from Ohio State University as an electrical and mechanical engineer. Among his accomplishments:

- Engineer at the National Cash Register Company—invented the electric cash register
- Invented the electric automobile starter for the 1912 Cadillac
- With friend E.A. Deeds, founded DELCO (Dayton Engineering Laboratories Co.)
- General Motors purchased DELCO in 1920, and "Boss Ket" became Vice President of General Motors Research
- Invented central air conditioning

The only son of Charles and Olive, Eugene Kettering graduated from Cornell University and was associated with projects that contributed to the development of the diesel engine. For many years he was active in research projects with General Motors.

When Eugene and his wife, Virginia, moved to Hinsdale, Illinois, in 1938, God's hand was guiding the process. Charles Kettering often visited his son and family in Hinsdale, and, ever the philanthropist, became interested in and gave generously to several institutions in and around Hinsdale, including the Hinsdale Sanitarium and Hospital, a Seventh-day Adventist hospital.

It was during the hot, muggy summer of 1949 that a young boy in the Kettering's neighborhood was stricken with the dreaded polio, sending chills throughout the community. There were no adequate facilities in the suburbs of Chicago for treating polio at the time, and the boy was sent elsewhere for treatment.

Soon other cases erupted in the community—as many as 53 in one three-week period—making obvious the desperate need for local treatment. The Ketterings purchased and donated eight iron lungs to help with the more acute cases. Slowly, the epidemic ended, but this frightening experience kindled a new interest in expanding and modernizing Hinsdale Sanitarium.

The Ketterings gave the first $1,000,000 to the fund raising drive. The total of $4,000,000 for the hospital expansion was soon realized and on September 27, 1953, the ribbon signifying the opening of the enlarged hospital was cut by "Chucky" Richards, now a healthy eight-year-old boy, a former polio patient.

When his father died in 1958, Eugene and his wife Virginia moved back to Dayton to carry on the work of the Kettering Foundation. They announced their plans to build a major hospital there as a memorial to their father, to be located on the Charles F. Kettering estate. They donated 80 of the 90 acres of the father's property, including Ridgeleigh Terrace, the historic Kettering home, which just incidentally was the first home in the United States to have central air conditioning.

They recalled their close association with the Hinsdale Sanitarium, and had been especially impressed with the service and character of the institution. So they made the decision to offer this great memorial to the Seventh-day Adventist Church, adding it to the chain of more than 100 Adventist hospitals, many of which they had visited all over the world.

Virginia Kettering took her friend, the widow of Lee Harrison, a former Vice-president of General Motors, on a tour through the hospital during an early phase of the construction. "This building really needs a fourth floor to give us the possibility for expansion," she told her friend.

"Well, if you'll call it the Harrison Pavilion, I'll pay for half," she told Mrs. Kettering.

"Wonderful; I'll pay for the other half and we'll soon have the fourth floor—the Harrison Pavilion," Virginia replied happily.

On March 3, 1964, the first patients were admitted to Kettering Memorial Hospital—nine of them. But the next year saw more than 11,000 patients admitted and more than 1,000 births. Kettering Medical Center Network (KMCN) now includes five hospitals (Kettering, Sycamore, Grandview, Southview and Greene Memorial Hospital) and 51 satellite facilities in the Dayton area. KMCN has 7,000 employees, and in a recent year saw more than 20,000 admissions. Kettering College of Medical Arts which opened in 1967 and shares the Kettering campus, has more than 900 students in a variety of healthcare fields.

"Today the Kettering Medical Center Network ... emphasizes excellence and innovation in medical care while still embracing God's love."

Today the Kettering Medical Center Network is a comprehensive, non-profit, faith-based healthcare network that emphasizes excellence and innovation in medical care while still embracing God's love—treating patients with compassion, kindness, and respect in the spirit of the global Seventh-day Adventist healthcare ministry. Four of the Network's hospitals rank in the top 100 among the 5,000 hospitals in the United States. In 2010, for the second year in a row the Kettering Health Network was recognized by Thomson Reuters as one of the top ten health systems in the nation.

God and some of His friends are helping multitudes find health. For nearly a half century Dr. Vernon Luthas has been an integral part of that mission.

"For all the promises of God in Him are Yes, and in Him Amen, to the glory of God through us." 2 Corinthians 1:20 NKJV

After Dr. Vernon had been at Kettering Hospital for four years, he received a different kind of phone call, this one also from Dr. Harley Rice of the General Conference Medical Department. It seems there was an urgent need for a skilled anesthesiologist at the Bella Vista (pronounced bay-a veesta) Hospital in Puerto Rico. Would Vernon come and help them?

He and Betty prayed, weighed options, paced the floor. And prayed. Vern was just getting his practice to the strong place he wanted it to be. Kettering Hospital had state-of-the-art facilities, his and Betty's closest friends were there, and he was making a comfortable living for his family. Their children were in an excellent school environment. It was about as pleasant a professional setting as one could wish.

However, their lifelong dream had been to serve in a mission setting, and Bella Vista needed them. Almost before they began to pray about the call they had sensed God's will. The next day they phoned Harley Rice to tell him they would go. It would be the first of a dozen years spent outside the United States in places including Puerto Rico, Penang, Malaysia, Japan, and Curacao.

Vern knew from personal experience that you can trust that what God promised He would fulfill.

"For all the promises of God in Him are Yes, and in Him Amen, to the glory of God through us." 2 Corinthians 1:20 NKJV

– Chapter 4 –

A Mountain? Stamp it "Moved!"

As we left Vernon and Betty so we could explore the beginning of Kettering Memorial Hospital, they had just hung up the phone and were packing boxes, getting ready to head to Puerto Rico.

Puerto Rico is a lovely green jewel in the sun, and part of the Greater Antilles chain in the Mediterranean Sea. It is 119 miles wide and 35 miles from north to south, slightly smaller than the state of Rhode Island.

An east-west mountain range dominates the topography, and although it has no long rivers or major lakes it's a lush tropical island. When you think of mid-20th century Puerto Rico you may picture a tropical paradise with palm trees, gorgeous flowers, succulent fruits, beckoning beaches; all are true. But there was also the reality of the difficult day-to-day. Bella Vista Hospital is a mission hospital, and those who worked there had become accustomed to hardships.

As you can guess, the weather was often sultry and oppressive in Puerto Rico and the air conditioner in the window of the little campus house assigned to the Luthases was temperamental at best. In fact, it seemed to work on its own schedule. The phone in the house must have been designed by the same company because it seldom worked either. With cell phones not yet available, Vernon found himself making innumerable trips across the hospital grounds, often in the middle of the night, to see if one of his patients needed care. However, despite the obstacles, this community became a place of miracles.

But let's rewind a bit and discover how God planted a church and a hospital in Mayaguez, Puerto Rico.

Earlier in its history the chief crop of the island was sugar. During the Second World War, Dr. William Dunscombe was recruited from the College of Medical Evangelists (in Loma Linda) because a physician was desperately needed on the west end of the island. His assignment was to meet the medical needs of the large colony of sugar cane workers. There was no hospital, so Dr. Dunscombe set up a little house and called it the Dunscombe Clinic; here he could keep patients who needed more than out-patient care.

After his work for the sugar mill company, Dr. Dunscombe saw opportunity for a larger ministry and moved to Mayaguez, the largest city on the west end of the island. There he assisted in the construction of a small Seventh-day Adventist church. In 1954 he opened a clinic on the mountain just above the city, the forerunner of what would become Bella Vista Adventist Hospital.

Other medical missionaries would join Dr. Dunscombe and soon a larger clinic with the capability of serving a wide range of medical needs was opened. The American Seventh-day Adventist doctors were seeing larger and larger numbers of patients. They were excellent physicians and their skills soon began attracting patients from ever larger parts of the island. Predictably, this success created some problems.

As the local physicians saw it, these American doctors spelled trouble for two reasons—political and financial. Mayaguez was the hub of a movement that desired to retain political independence. Local residents were suspicious that the Americans might intend to influence the future of the island's government. They could see the island, under American prodding, quickly moving from a territory to a commonwealth and they wanted none of it.

"God planted a church and a hospital in Mayaguez, Puerto Rico."

Also, they could envision these highly-trained and successful physicians as a threat to their livelihoods. They were "the competition." So the Americans were perceived as the enemy by a majority of the Puerto Rican doctors.

Meanwhile, the medical work at Bella Vista was growing. The little hospital was bulging at the seams. There seemed to be patients everywhere, often in the halls. And as its popularity increased, so did the tension between the physicians on the medical staff and hospital leadership. The American physicians couldn't carry the increasing load alone, but the non-SDA physicians seemed determined to undermine their influence.

In 1978 Frank Perez was asked to return from the United States to his wife's Puerto Rican homeland as hospital administrator at Bella Vista. He had been working successfully in New Jersey, and knew that the situation in Mayaguez would be a contrast to what he was leaving behind. Cuban by birth, many of the professional people on the island were not ready to accept Bella Vista's new leadership, and Frank often found himself persona non grata on the island. To further complicate matters, just as Frank was arriving, two severe hurricanes swept the island—Hurricane David and Hurricane Frederick, leaving chaos and even more medical needs in their wake.

"As he shared the challenges with Vernon, he said, 'My friend, I believe that you and God are the only ones who can save this hospital.'"

Quickly assessing his new responsibilities, Frank saw two major trouble spots in the hospital—the Emergency Room and the Anesthesia department. Both were woefully short-staffed and under-equipped. There were no Adventist anesthesiologists, and a group of antagonistic nationals seemed to have taken over that part of the hospital's work. Many of the physicians were threatening to take their patients elsewhere, especially the pediatricians, since their need for anesthesiologists was so acute. This loss of clientele could tip the scales and mean the death knell for the hospital.

Perez had sought help and a call was extended to Vernon Luthas in Ohio. Perez himself was working on a very minimal "missionary pastor's salary," and he couldn't offer Dr. Luthas much more than that. But there was an urgent need and that captured the mission spirit of the Luthases. Frank knew that Dr. Luthas was a successful and respected anesthesiologist at Kettering Hospital and would be a strong addition to their team.

As he shared the challenges with Vernon, he said, "My friend, I believe that you and God are the only ones who can save this hospital." Vernon listened and could see the enormous needs. He talked to Betty and to his anesthesia partners who would need to carry some of his work while he was away. A day later he called Frank to say that they would be coming. The call was processed quickly through the Inter-American Division of the church, and Vern and Betty were underway. They would spend a year in Puerto Rico on this first assignment; ten years total.

Vernon sensed huge battles ahead because he knew that the national physicians wanted the hospital closed and all the Americans to be gone. When the Luthases arrived, the nationals were caught off guard. They couldn't call Vernon a "paleface." As a Chinese, he was not exactly what they had expected. Besides, he spoke fluent Spanish. And Vernon had another huge advantage—his spiritual strength.

They could not have anticipated his sweet spirit. If one of them refused to take an emergency case in the middle of the night you would see Dr. Vernon, trudging from his warm bed across the lawn to the hospital. No matter how tired, he never complained, he just quietly did the work that needed to be done, not because he was paid to do it but because it was the right thing to do.

An ominous threat was hanging over Bella Vista Hospital. They were facing the almost certain loss of their accreditation, which was a very serious possibility. This would mean that they would be perceived in the community as an unsafe, substandard facility and they would not qualify to receive Medicare patients. In this area of the island most of the patients' hospitalization costs were covered by Medicare. The most critical area, and the one with the most serious infractions, was the anesthesia department.

Chief of Surgery Dr. Ray Nelson was a friend and classmate of Vernon's. Very soon after Vern arrived, Dr. Nelson asked him to do whatever needed to be done to the department so that it would pass inspection. As Vernon studied the situation it seemed an impossible task. Vern accepted the responsibility humbly as an assignment from the Lord, but reminded the Lord continually that he was depending on divine help in this crisis.

He soon discovered that the hurdles were more acute than he had been told. First, he himself had to have a license to practice medicine in Puerto Rico. The Puerto Rican government accepted his degree from the College of Medical Evangelists; that had already been established. But he would soon discover that they would not give him the necessary papers to practice medicine here. Their law said that anyone who was not a resident of Puerto Rico must work a year for the government before being granted a license. But there was no time for that now; he needed to start work immediately.

Vernon sensed God's leading him to share this latest obstacle with his friend, Fred Hernandez, Chaplain at the hospital. They prayed together, then almost eagerly Fred suggested that he would be willing to talk to the Judge in San Juan. The interesting ingredient in the story is this: the Judge was Fred's brother!

In the Hebrew language, the language in which the Old Testament scriptures were primarily written, there is no word in that vocabulary for "coincidence." The Hebrew people had come to understand that the providence of God was so strong that when events occurred that seemed irregular it was not accidental or happenstance, but the wise leading of an omnipotent God. Vernon was about to see that fact in full color.

As the little group visited with Fred's brother and laid out the problem, the Judge replied that they could work around the problem. Vernon could be granted a professional internship, be licensed as an intern, and at the end of one year, be granted a full license to practice. Another mountain moved. God's provision proved sufficient again. He does go before us and He does prepare the way. Years before this crisis developed, God had put the pieces in place to solve it.

"I will go before you and prepare the way. I will break down gates of brass and crash through iron bars." Isaiah 45:2, 3

"I will go before you and prepare the way. I will break down gates of brass and crash through iron bars." Isaiah 45:2, 3

Frank Perez, the hospital Administrator, was thankful for Vern's professional presence, even though he could pay Vern a stipend of only $500/month. Vernon knew that he was where God wanted him to be and set to work to discover problems and to help the department meet the standards for the Joint Commission on Accreditation of Hospitals.

He had only three months to re-write hospital policies and prepare the department to meet the stringent requirements. Vernon called his good friend and partner, Dean Johnson, because they had just gone through the accreditation process at the Kettering Hospital. Dean sent all the paperwork necessary immediately so Vernon could get started.

"Each time a question came up, Vern turned to one of his folders and produced information that satisfied the examiner."

Dr. Vernon worked feverishly day and night for those three months and at the time of the inspection visit, he had 13 file folders crammed with solutions to issues he knew the Accreditation team would raise. Most of the infractions had been addressed, and the work was either finished or well-started in all of these 13 areas. Except. ... Except there were two on the list that he hadn't been able to solve.

At 7:00 AM on the day of the inspection Vernon met with the physician from the Joint Commission on Accreditation of Hospitals (JCAH), who seemed to have come with the mind-set that it was not going to happen for the Bella Vista Hospital

Anesthesia Department to pass inspection that day.

But what the visiting inspector probably didn't realize was that there was an unseen Guest who met with them that morning. As Dr. Luthas introduced himself, the inspecting physician was caught off guard and was very interested in his name. "Luthas is not a Chinese name," he said. "Are you Chinese?" Vernon assured him that he was.

"My best friend is a Chinese physician. His name is Julio Wong and he is from Panama."

Now Vern was the surprised one! His parents were friends of Julio Wong's parents in Panama, and now he and the physician from JCAH had some common ground. The inspector wanted to know about Vern's background, so Vern told him that he had been born at Gorgas Hospital in Panama. This broke the ice, and they shared stories and common interests. Instead of a cold, matter-of-fact inspection, Vern found himself at ease, discussing problems with a new friend who now gave evidence that he wanted to help.

After a friendly visit, the inspector said, "Well, we'd better do the work I came to do. I have some questions here."

Each time a question came up, Vern turned to one of his folders and produced information that satisfied the examiner. After two hours, all the folders were empty, and Vern was praying for wisdom, not knowing where the conversation might go from there. He had no more folders.

"I have one more question, but we've spent two hours, we've gone into great detail … and I just forgot the last question," said the examiner. He could see that Vern had done his work thoroughly, and he was satisfied.

As the examiner gave his report at the end of the day, he said, "I met a man today from Panama who has done a remarkable job in meeting the requirements in the Anesthesia Department. There are still some issues to be dealt with, but we are pleased to give you a three-year accreditation."

A mountain? Stamp it "Moved!"

God knew. It is not difficult to believe that when you reflect on this journey. He had been preparing Vernon for this day, even when Vernon's grandparents came from China in 1903. He had a plan for them, and for their children. When Vern's parents were married, his mother's family was not happy about her marrying an "older man." Vern's father was 35; his mother was 18 but her faith in God set the spiritual tone for the entire family. The Dunns went to Panama as missionaries and were instrumental in bringing the Luthas boys to the U.S. Their father's illness brought the family together again in southern California. Two friendly Chinese medical students nudged Vernon in the direction of a career in medicine. The examiner who came to Bella Vista that day was from Panama. He and Vernon shared mutual friends. Maybe it's true in English also that there really is no such word as "coincidence."

– Chapter 5 –

Expensive Expansion

Had you seen the Bella Vista Hospital at this time in its life, you would probably have shaken your head and come away with the impression: Now I understand what "full and running over" means. The hospital was experiencing an unusually high census, producing very crowded conditions. Not surprisingly, their overworked and worn-out facilities were breaking down. Much of the physical plant was outdated and long past its prime.

The main trouble spots were the intensive care unit, the nursery, and the operating rooms. At the very places where they should have been able to do their best work, and where the patients' needs were most acute, they were falling short. It was a stressful time but they knew what to do—they took it to the Lord.

God gave the promise that really seemed to fit their difficulty:

"Do not fear, for you will not be ashamed, nor be disgraced." Isaiah 54:4

Another verse from the pen of King David that gave great hope:

"Call upon Me in the day of trouble; I will deliver you and you shall glorify Me." Psalm 50:15

The needs were critical, and they felt like Hudson Taylor, the great man of faith who established the Inland China Mission. Though he was virtually penniless the Lord always provided for his needs. Taylor commented, when asked about the status of the finances for his extensive work, "I have 25 cents and all the promises of God."

They had a choice—they could focus on their circumstances, which were dismal, or look to their God, whose resources are inexhaustible. They chose to look up. They knew He was aware of their urgent needs. So they took their specific problems to Him, laid them all out before Him, and reminded Him of the commitments He had made in His Word. They committed their plans to Him. They had nowhere else to turn, so they gave Him everything. And they found reassurance in His word:

"Commit to the Lord whatever you do, and your plans will succeed." Proverbs 16:3 NIV

"He does not ignore the prayers of those in trouble when they call to Him for help." Psalm 9:12 TLB

The original plans when the hospital tower addition had been built included operating rooms, intensive care, and nurseries, but now two floors of the new tower had become a ghost town—quiet, unfinished, abandoned. The work had stopped because there were no funds to finish. The two quiet, dark floors were a framed-in reminder of what should have been, nothing more.

As the new Administrator, Frank Perez, and his friend, Dr.

Vernon, studied the problem and met to pray, they brought to God two main dilemmas: they had been unable to find just the right architects to design the interiors of the floors, and they needed funds to finish them.

They spread it out before God as Hezekiah did when he took his threatening letter to the temple to pray. Then Dr. Luthas contacted his friends back home and told them about the problem. Before long, two outstanding architects came to their rescue, traveling to Mayaguez at their own expense. Over a period of weeks they painstakingly drew up plans for state-of-the-art operating rooms, an intensive care unit, and nurseries.

> ***"He does not ignore the prayers of those in trouble when they call to Him for help."***
> **Psalm 9:12 TLB**

If blueprints can be beautiful, these were gorgeous! The architects had thought of everything! Frank and his team were thrilled with the quality. But what would it cost to pay these architects who came with a specialty in hospital design? Actually, they came as volunteers, glad to do all of their work on a pro bono basis!

God had surprised the hospital team once again in a way they hadn't anticipated. When the architects left Puerto Rico they had the great satisfaction of knowing they had filled a glaring need. They knew they were cooperating with Someone greater than they could imagine, the Master Designer Himself.

Now Frank Perez, Dr. Luthas, and others turned their attention to making the blueprints a reality. It would cost an estimated $400,000 to finish the construction; the total in the bank they knew exactly: $0. So again they went to their knees to talk to the One who owns the worlds. This was a comfortable habit for them. They prayed, and worked, and trusted—needing and expecting. It became a daily way of life. They took their priceless plans to Him and told Him what they needed next.

They reminded Him it was for Him, for His work, and they relied on words like:

"The work is of God, and He will furnish means, and will send helpers." Desire of Ages, p. 370

And this statement fit their circumstances as it has encouraged so many of God's children in similar times of need:

"The means in our possession may not seem to be sufficient for the work; but if we will move forward in faith, believing in the all-sufficient power of God, abundant resources will open before us." Desire of Ages, p. 371

They needed those "abundant resources," and as soon as possible. At that time the amount loomed much more ominously than it might today. Milton Murray, from the General Conference Development office, was the first to come to their aid. He had visited Bella Vista before, and was eager to be of help again. His expertise and experience were invaluable. He rolled up his sleeves and tackled the job with characteristic skill and wisdom.

Perez and Murray worked together, contacting people in Puerto Rico, giving them an opportunity to assist financially, and the people responded. Hundreds had a part in raising the money. Physicians chipped in, employees purchased bricks and some even took mortar and "set" their bricks in a space that was waiting for them in the new expansion. It was exciting to see that people from the community, the church, and the hospital were taking ownership and responsibility for the success of "their" hospital. Most had never had this kind of adventure before, but they knew they were doing something big that would provide better health care for their patients, their family, and their neighbors.

It was like the Bible story when the people "had a mind to work," (Nehemiah 4:6)and before long they had their new, splendid and well-equipped facilities, some of the best to be found anywhere. And perhaps the most amazing part of the story—the entire project was completed without ever having to borrow one dollar!

"The work is of God, and He will furnish means, and will send helpers." Desire of Ages, p. 370

Alas, the new structure was completed, but empty. A beautiful addendum to the story is how God provided necessary medical equipment. Multiple tons of needed instruments, equipment, and supplies were donated and shipped by Dr. Luthas' friends at Kettering Hospital. Beds and other hospital furniture came for other hospital units, providing needed upgrades. It was like Christmas on steroids—opening crates and containers and boxes of much-needed items. It gave Bella Vista a brand new look!

As the hospital family was increasing, the church family was growing too, and their little church was soon woefully inadequate for the numbers of people of all ages who were appearing each week. God was adding to that group too. In order to build a new structure they knew that it would have to be a team effort. On Sundays you might find Frank Perez, Vernon Luthas, and many others, physicians, and employees from every hospital department building the church, doing things they didn't know they could do.

This was the only way they could have a new church. It was definitely a do-it-ourselves project. But just as God gave special talents, and gifted specific people for their tasks in building the tabernacle in the wilderness, He gave special help to the builders of His house in Mayaguez, Puerto Rico.

Torrential Rain

When it came time to pour concrete for the foundations, the island was in the middle of the rainy season, when it rains every day. But they couldn't stop. They had to press forward. When they contacted the concrete company, they were told to "forget it," it was impossible to pour concrete in the rain.

So the members of the congregation came together on the Thursday night before they needed to do the pour and again laid out their case before the Lord. They reminded Him of the promises in His Word. They reminded Him that this was for Him, and they really needed His intervention now.

"Present your case', says the Lord. 'Bring forth your strong reasons,' says the King of Jacob."

They pleaded with God to withhold the rain the next day, Friday. They were trusting in the One who had given them His word, and they knew that nothing is impossible with God. Just as He had done for His children in the wilderness, God gave His children on that mountain in Bella Vista great faith to ask their God to hold back what everyone new was inevitable.

They called the concrete contractor, but he didn't want to come. He thought it was foolhardy, but they insisted and finally convinced him that he should at least come to the site and bring his crew on Friday morning. So he agreed "just to check," but he was prepared to leave because there was no doubt in his mind—it was going to rain.

Friday morning and afternoon there was no rain. None. Zero.

"Friday morning and afternoon there was no rain. None. Zero."

From their position on the mountain, the workers could see the rain all around them, but it didn't rain on their mountain that day. So the contractor and his crew poured concrete all morning and all afternoon. As they finished, the foreman smiled as he looked up into the sky, and said, "Well, we're finished; it can rain now." Within ten minutes the rain began.

There was a hush over God's people as they realized what their Creator had done for them that day. It's a humbling experience to see God move in answer to the prayers of His people. They learned something that day they would long remember—we have a God who responds to the faith and the needs of His children. Even though He is mighty and awesome, sovereign and omnipotent, yet he is the gentle Shepherd who cares for His own. He is always there. Always.

The Cherokee Indians have a legend that helps illustrate that truth. It concerns the rite of passage for their youth:

When the boy is 12 his father takes him deep into the forest, blindfolds him, and leaves him alone. He is required to sit on a stump the entire night and not remove the blindfold until the rays of the morning sun appear. He cannot cry out for help to anyone and he must vow not to tell the other boys of his experience because each must come into manhood on his own.

The boy is naturally terrified. He can hear all the night sounds in the forest. Wild horses may be near. Wolves may be on the hunt. Coyotes howl in the distance. Maybe even some human might discover him there and do him harm. The wind blows the grass and branches and shakes his stump, but he sits stoically, never removing the blindfold. It is the only way he can become a man!

Finally, after an agonizing night, the sun appears and he removes his blindfold. It is only then he discovers his father sitting on the stump next to him. He had been at watch the entire night, protecting his son from harm.

"It is only then he discovers his father sitting on the stump next to him. He had been at watch the entire night, protecting his son from harm."

We too, are never alone. Even when we don't know it, even when it doesn't feel like it, even when we can't see Him, God is watching over us, sitting on the "stump" beside us. Because we can't see Him doesn't mean he isn't there.

Losing a Leg

Just before returning to Kettering from his first year at Bella Vista Hospital, Vernon encountered a very unique patient. The man had been to the hospital for surgery before and had done well, but this time he was coming for a leg amputation. He was 108. Vern's oldest patient previously had been a woman who was 93, so he wanted to have the honor of giving the anesthesia for this centenarian even though he knew it would be a difficult case. In the employ of the Great Physician Dr. Vernon was never reluctant to tackle the tough assignments. Because he knew God was at his side, he was eager for any challenge.

One of the nurses laughingly told the patient, "You're older than this hospital!"

"I'm also older than the dirt it's built on," the patient replied with a 100-year-old twinkle in his eye. Incidentally, the patient did well and once again had as uncomplicated a recovery as a 108-year-old patient can have after very major surgery.

– Chapter 6 –

No Wonder They Call it Amazing

A life that honors God does not often consist of a rapid sequence of heroic events. In fact, history demonstrates that most of God's heroes don't even get their picture in the paper; they're seldom seen on the 10:00 news. A life that honors God is more likely to be punctuated by consistent exhibits of His grace, often in unexpected places.

In His delightful book, "Putting a Face on Grace," Richard Blackaby challenges us to see the magnitude of what God desires to do through us. He says, "We can persuade the world of the validity of our message by the way we demonstrate grace ... grace is a magnetic force that draws people to God, the source of grace."

Dr. Vern has cultivated a sensitivity to the feelings and needs of others. He has made it a life goal to seek out, to search for, those he can help. Someone has said that in the game of life, many of us who cross home plate do so because we were fortunate enough to be born on third base. Vernon recognizes those who were not born on third base and looks for ways to do everything he can to help them run the bases too.

"Success depends not so much on talent as on energy and willingness. It is not the possession of splendid talents that enables us to render acceptable service, but the conscientious performance of daily duties, the contented spirit, the unaffected, sincere interest in the welfare of others."
Prophets & Kings p. 219

The rescue of a friend

Vernon became aware of a friend whom we'll call Dr. Charles, an anesthesiologist, who had just been let go from his position in the prestigious hospital where he had worked for nearly 25 years. Charles was 50-plus years of age and felt he had nowhere to go. Distraught and feeling that he had hit bottom, his situation seemed hopeless. Vern discovered that Dr. Charles was in trouble and invited him to come and work with him and his partners. Some of the others in the anesthesia group were reluctant to bring him on board, but Vernon went out on a limb for him.

"At his memorial service many years later, his son would tell the friends who were there, 'Dr. Luthas saved my father's life.'"

The group finally agreed and Charles was taken on as a partner. The newcomer was cautious and frequently sought advice from Vernon. If he was feeling insecure about a specific case Vern would swap with him, giving him a patient with fewer probable complications. Vern quietly mentored Charles and helped him develop his best qualities. Charles' confidence grew and he stayed on and worked successfully in the group for nearly 20 years until he retired. Vern's kindness was not lost on Charles or his family. At his memorial service many years later, his son would tell the friends who were there, "Dr. Luthas saved my father's life."

Crisis at sea

Vernon's brother Carlton and his wife, Clara, had been through some difficult and heart-rending difficulties. Clara was diagnosed with cancer and had gone through a long and grueling regimen of chemotherapy. The chemo had not been kind; she had lost her hair, her skin had broken down in unsightly and painful blisters and sores. She wore long sleeves to hide what she felt was ugly.

Carlton and Clara were delighted when Vernon offered to take them on a Caribbean cruise—their first, and just at the time when they both needed a boost. Vern and Betty also invited their friends, Jack and Barb Fritzsche, and their daughter, Robin, and the seven had a great adventure. The men carried Clara's wheelchair when necessary and made sure that she didn't miss any of the fun. They even took boat rides (from the ocean liner to shore). They wanted her to have it all, and she loved them for it.

One evening at dinner the five of them waited for Carlton and Clara, but they didn't join them at the table as usual. Vern excused himself and went quickly to their cabin.

As he knocked at their door, he prayed for wisdom. He knew that it had been a happy, yet difficult trip for his brother and sister-in-law. When Carlton opened the door, Vern could see that both he and his wife were in tears.

Clara had glimpsed herself in the bathroom mirror. She realized again how much the cancer and the chemotherapy had taken from her, and she was devastated. She looked at her pale and pocked skin, her sunken eyes, and in her weakened state suddenly it was just too much. She couldn't face going to dinner "looking like this." Vern listened and he hurt for them. But he knew he could not fix it. "Let's pray," he said.

Vernon and his brother knelt beside Clara's wheelchair in that room, giving the problem to God. The Lord's presence was sweet that night, lifting a huge burden. Both Carlton and Clara invited Christ into their hearts at a deeper and more empowering level. As Clara gave the burden to the Lord, He took it, and she never again was plagued with the overwhelming sense of discouragement. Vernon says, "The Lord changed the atmosphere in that room that night." God had whispered His peace to her heart and blessed all three as Vernon had prayed.

A changed life

One of his colleagues, Dr. Peter, a physician in another department in the hospital, had become a problem to Vern. Dr. Peter was consistently caustic, surly, difficult to deal with, and because this is the opposite of Vernon's nature, he often found the man unpleasant to be around. If he had no reason to be with him, he avoided him.

Maybe this little internet story from an unknown author describes Dr. Peter:

One day I hopped in a taxi and we took off for the

airport. We were driving in the right lane when suddenly a black car jumped out of a parking space right in front of us. My taxi driver slammed on his brakes, skidded, and missed the other car by just inches. The driver of the other car whipped his head around and started yelling at us.

My taxi driver just smiled and waved at the guy. And I mean, he was really friendly. So I asked, 'Why did you just do that? This guy almost ruined your car and sent us to the hospital!'

This is when my taxi driver taught me what I now call The Law of the Garbage Truck. He explained that many people are like garbage trucks. They run around full of garbage, full of frustration, full of anger, full of disappointment.

As their garbage piles up, they need a place to dump it and sometimes they'll dump it on you. Don't take it personally.

"It is only then he discovers his father sitting on the stump next to him. He had been at watch the entire night, protecting his son from harm."

Just smile, wave, wish them well, and move on. Don't take their garbage and spread it to other people at work, at home, or on the streets.

The bottom line is that successful people do not let garbage trucks take over their day. Life is too short to wake up in the morning with regrets, so love the people who treat you right. Pray for the ones who don't.

Vern knew that Dr. Peter was unhappy, but sometimes he could be so vitriolic and unpleasant it was just easier to dodge a bitter experience. One Sunday evening at a concert Vernon found himself actually relieved when Dr. Peter came in and found a seat some rows away instead of sitting next to him. However after the program was over and Vern was driving home he sensed the Lord confronting him about his feelings. Vernon felt that he must go see Dr. Peter and try to help him.

The next morning, driving to their home a few miles away he wondered what he would say, and as he always did, he asked the Lord for help. When Vern arrived he was disappointed to find that the man was not there. He waited and talked with the family, hoping that Dr. Peter would return, but after about an hour he decided to leave. Maybe he had misunderstood God's directions. But Dr. Peter's wife said, "Please don't go, Vernon. He just went out for a short walk, and should be right back."

"Vernon was here and prayed with me again. That man's prayers get through to heaven."

About that time Dr. Peter entered his house by the back door. When he saw Vernon, he shouted, "What are you doing here?" Vern tried to tell him that he had just stopped by to visit. But again, the other doctor yelled, "I said, What Are You Doing Here?" Vern tried calmly to explain that he had stopped by for a visit. For the third time, Dr. Peter raised his voice and exploded, "WHAT ARE

YOU DOING HERE?"

"I have come to see you, Peter." Vernon said. I wanted to tell you that I want no hard feelings between us, I want to be your friend and I want to do anything I can for you."

Dr. Peter, stunned, broke down and began to sob. They were all crying as Peter told Vernon and his family that he had taken a gun with him that day as he went for his walk in the woods. He didn't plan to return, but somehow God broke through to his depressed mind with a sense of urgency to return to his home. When he saw Dr. Luthas there, he knew that God must be trying to save his life.

Vernon asked if they could pray, and as the family knelt together Dr. Peter saw a ray of hope. The Great Physician was there in that circle as He had promised. Peter thanked Vernon for saving his life. God had let light shine into his abject darkness that day.

The next day Vernon was again impressed to go to Dr. Peter's office there in the hospital, just to follow up on their visit the night before. Vern seldom had time between his anesthesia cases, but that day he had a few minutes and the Lord impressed him to go and check on his friend.

As he entered the office he could see that Peter was again feeling depressed. Again they prayed together. After Vernon left, Peter phoned his wife and told her, "Vernon was here and prayed with me again. That man's prayers get through to heaven. I feel so much better. God seems to keep telling me that with Him there are no hopeless cases—not even me."

Although Peter has died in the intervening years, his wife will always remember the times God used His humble servant to minister to her struggling husband and get him back to emotional stability when no one else seemed able to reach him.

If we consider those around us as fellow life travelers all in need of grace as we are, we learn to see them differently. If there are people around you today who have been irritating or angering you, don't ask God to change them. Ask Him to adjust your perspective and make you an agent of His grace. It will radically transform your relationships. It isn't easy—that's why they call it Amazing.

Sometimes it's humanly impossible to forgive. Only God is loving and gracious enough to do that, but we can ask God to forgive someone through us. If they deserved it, it wouldn't be grace. God does miraculous work through ordinary people as He frees us from anger and bitterness and helps us forgive the unforgivable.

This is the amazing transaction in which God wants to involve us:

"If you have faith like this, you will lay hold upon God's word, and upon all the helpful agencies He has appointed. Thus your faith will strengthen, and will bring to your aid the power of heaven."
Desire of Ages p. 431

Behind the Scenes

Another "behind the scenes" story is a narrative of God's grace. When we pray for the ability to show grace to others, for patience, and for a sweet spirit, God often rolls out ample opportunities for us to practice. This was the case with Vernon's experience in the operating room with a prominent neurosurgeon. We're labeling it "behind the scenes" because, as He often does,

God solved the problem quietly.

Although Dr. Earl was a gifted neurosurgeon, Vernon and all those who worked with him were well aware of the trail of angry and hurt people left behind after one of his frequent tirades during surgery.

On one occasion when the case was extremely difficult and not going well, the air was filled with an almost palpable tension. No matter what anyone did, the patient was losing ground. On the operating table before them a young woman was fighting for her life—and losing.

As if things weren't bad enough, they suddenly took a huge turn for the worse as Dr. Earl began venting his industrial-strength venom with rudeness and cursing. He loudly demanded that no one talk. He didn't just command absolute silence, he demanded that everyone leave the room immediately—except Dr. Vernon, who was still working to keep the young patient alive.

"If you have faith like this, you will lay hold upon God's word, and upon all the helpful agencies He has appointed." Desire of Ages p. 431

When the staff had left, the surgeon again erupted, "Who is that talking?

Vernon, without even realizing it, had been praying. Even though he often prayed during surgery, this time he was praying softly aloud. He was telling the Lord that they were losing the patient, and he desperately needed the Lord's intervention.

"I am talking," Vernon replied. "I am praying because we need God's help here, and I know God is our only hope."

When Dr. Earl realized that it was Vernon, and that he had been praying for the outcome of the surgery, he was speechless. He stepped back from the patient and allowed Vernon to pray, and to do his work. God once again gave Vernon just the wisdom he needed to stabilize the patient. When her situation was safe, he told the surgeon he could continue the surgery.

The others returned, the case finished successfully, and the woman fully recovered. Everyone there that day was aware of God's miracle. Later Dr. Earl apologized to Vernon, and told him that the experience had changed his life. It was true, he became respectful toward his colleagues and left behind his emotional outbursts. "You can pray for me any time," he told Vern.

Showdown

Dr. Vernon's assurance, his confidence, come from his walk with God. His faith is in God's ability and he can say with Joshua, "The Lord is with us, do not be afraid."

His faith prepared him for an unexpected encounter with a world-renowned cardiac surgeon who came to join the medical staff at Kettering Medical Center.

His fame preceded him, and both the staff and others in the community were proud to have him on the team. It was considered something of a medical coup. He was not only an imminently successful heart surgeon, but had also developed the Bubble Oxygenator, a device that made open-heart surgical procedures possible.

For all his medical skills, however, the man was not a

believer and it irritated him that Dr. Luthas always prayed with his patients before surgery. At first he kept his discontent inside, but one day, unable to contain his irritation, he approached Dr. Vernon with a request.

"Vern, I notice that you always pray with my patients before surgery, and I would like to ask you not to pray with my patients in the future!"

"Well, Dick," Vernon replied, "these patients are mine, too, and this is an important part of my work so I must continue to do that."

Nothing more was said; the work atmosphere was congenial, and the two skilled physicians continued to work together. Dr. Vernon continued his practice of praying with all of his patients the evening before surgery, and again on the operating room table.

Years later this prominent heart surgeon would seek out Vern and say, "Vernon, I want to thank you for praying for my patients. Because of your prayers they really do seem to do better."

It takes a big man to acknowledge when he is wrong, and it takes a big God to open a strong man's heart. Now, long after retirement the two men remain good friends.

– Chapter 7 –

Kettering's Own Brother Benjamin

Even though Dr. Luthas has retired, his influence lives on in uncounted places on planet earth. The lives he touched are forever changed. Very early God gave him a purpose and a plan; He showed Vernon how important *people* are, and Vernon has lived his life driven by that message.

If you were to ask their vivacious daughter, Diane, about her father, she would tell you that her most important lessons from her father were not always taught, but caught. All her growing-up years, Diane watched as her father would go to see a struggling colleague, encourage someone, or help somebody in need. It didn't matter if they were in some out of the way places. People were important to him, and when he left, they knew they were respected and loved.

These familiar words were not just words to Vernon; they are a compass for his life:

"I shall pass this way but once. Therefore, any good that I can do or any kindness I can show let me do it now, for I shall not pass this way again."

"Some of my happiest memories as I was growing up," Diane says, " were trips we took as a family, and Dad and I would talk for long hours. He told me fascinating stories and taught me valuable lessons about relationships." She learned from him the importance of gratitude and of looking for the best in others. His influence is still prominent in her life. "I learned that people are important, not for what they can do for us, but for what we can do to make their lives a little better, " she recalls.

Victor Borge said that a laugh is the shortest distance between two people. Diane would tell you she believes it. She has a happy, sunny disposition—a trademark of the Luthas family.

Diane and her husband, OB-GYN specialist Dr. David Duocette, have three grown daughters of their own. Diane and David are keenly thankful for the sweet, powerful influence of Diane's father, not only in their own lives, but for their children. Their son, Richard, and his family also live in Dayton. Like his sister, his life has been richly blessed by his father's influence.

After retiring, Vern knew that God had not released him from his mandate to be the resident encourager wherever he was. He had seen the enormous difference that prayer made in the lives of those who were facing surgery. He remembered his patients who had slept peacefully the night before their procedure was to be done. They had smiled with a new calm after he had prayed. The prayers were a special gift and the patients knew it. Vernon knew the promise was true:

"You will keep him in perfect peace whose mind is stayed on You, because he trusts in You. Trust in the Lord forever, for in Jehovah, the Lord is everlasting strength." Isaiah 26: 3

Because prayer was a way of life with Vern, he wanted to see it continue as Kettering patients faced surgery. He prayed about and idea he believed God had given him, and he talked to some of his friends. He shared his dream with them, and before long they had organized a little group which they initially called simply "Prayer Partners."

This new informal cadre from many different denominations organized themselves into a team of pray-ers. They began regularly visiting patients before surgery to pray. God used them to bring hope. Their offers to pray were met with enthusiastic appreciation by the patients and their families from the community because of the precedent that had been set in the past.

"You will keep him in perfect peace whose mind is stayed on You, because he trusts in You. Trust in the Lord forever, for in Jehovah, the Lord is everlasting strength." Isaiah 26: 3

One woman wrote to the hospital administration, describing how very fearful she had been as she approached her surgery the next morning, and that when someone came to pray with her she was literally shaking with fright. As the prayer partner introduced himself and asked if she would like for him to pray for her, she quickly agreed. She later would explain that somehow during the prayer she was able to turn her fears over to God and to know that she would not be alone.

In his prayer the visitor prayed for her by name and asked for wisdom for the surgeon and those who would be assisting.

She was able to face the surgery with peace. Her letter closed by saying, "I can walk today because of that surgery."

So the legacy continues. The prayer initiative program has expanded to become an integral part of the spiritual ministry provided by Kettering Medical Center Network.

Winston Baldwin is pastor of the Centerville Seventh-day Adventist Church where Vernon is a member. Pastor Baldwin says that in his large church of over 600 members, he has one very influential, outstanding member who prefers to work underground, anonymously, but as he spreads the living water around, the garden that is growing is beautiful.

"... he wants no applause or medals. He is simply living his life for others, and is still making a difference."

That member is a retired anesthesiologist who tries to remain anonymous; he wants no applause or medals. He is simply living his life for others, and is still making a difference. His "conspiracy of kindness" is contagious. He really believes and lives by the truth that "the kingdom advances among friends."

He may buy new books for the church library, he may pay so that a member can attend a training conference, he keeps an astute eye on the church entrance on Sabbath morning looking for guests he can welcome—and invite to dinner at his home.

Why? After all, he's a full-time caregiver at home. Perhaps it's because he understands that ministry is something *everyone* can do, no matter the age or circumstances.

You may have read the fascinating fable, *Finding Brother Benjamin*. There are parallels that remind us of the life of Vernon Luthas. Here's the powerful little story:

"Unfavorable winds blew the ship off course, and when they did the sailors spotted uncharted islands. They see half a dozen mounds rising out of the blue South Seas waters. The captain orders the men to drop anchor and goes ashore. He is a robust man with a barrel chest, full beard, and curious soul.

On the first island he sees nothing but sadness. Underfed children. Tribes in conflict. No farming or food development, no treatment for the sick, and no schools. Just simple, needy people.

The second and following islands reveal more of the same. The captain sighs at what he sees. "This is no life for these people. But what can he do?"

Then he steps onto the last and largest island. The people are healthy and well fed.

Irrigation systems nourish their fields, and roads connect the villages. The children have bright eyes and strong bodies. The captain asks the chief for an explanation. How has this island moved so far ahead of the others?

The chief, who is smaller than the captain but every bit his equal in confidence, gives a quick response: "Brother Benjamin. He educated us in everything from agriculture to health. He built schools and clinics and dug wells."

The captain asks, "Can you take me to see him?"

The chief nods and signals for two tribesmen to join

him. They guide the captain over a jungle ridge to a simple, expansive medical clinic. It is equipped with clean beds and staffed with trained caretakers. They show the captain the shelves of medicine and introduce him to the staff. The captain, though impressed, sees nothing of Brother Benjamin. "Can you take me to where he lives?"

The three natives looked puzzled. They confer among themselves. After several minutes the chief invites, "Follow us to the other side of the island." They walk along the shoreline until they reach a series of fishponds. Canals connect the ponds to the ocean. As the tide rises, fish pass from the ocean into the ponds. The islanders then lower canal gates and trap the fish for harvest.

Again the captain is amazed. He meets fishermen and workers, gatekeepers and net casters. But he sees nothing of Brother Benjamin. He wonders if he is making himself clear.

"I don't see Brother Benjamin. Please take me to where he lives," he repeats.

The trio talks alone again. After some discussion the chief offers, "Let us go up the mountain." They lead the captain up a steep, narrow path. After many twists and turns the path brings them out in front of a grass-roofed chapel. The voice of the chief is soft and earnest. "'He has taught us about God."

He escorts the captain inside and shows him the altar, a pulpit, a cross, several rows of benches, and a Bible.

"Is this where Brother Benjamin lives?" the captain asks.

The men nod and smile.

"May I talk to him?"

Their faces grow suddenly serious. "Oh, that would be impossible."

"Why?"

"He died many years ago."

The bewildered captain stares at the men. "I asked to see him, and you showed me a clinic, some fish farms, and the chapel. You said nothing of his death."

"You didn't ask about his death," the chief explains. "You asked to see where he lives. We showed you."

Outlive Your Life—Max Lucado

– Chapter 8 –

Did You Know?

George Nelson

George Nelson and his wife, Elsa, came to the Kettering Hospital project from Glendale, California, where he had served as administrator of the Glendale Sanitarium and Hospital. His experience as a successful administrator was helpful, but this was an entirely different kind of assignment. Here the mission was to oversee the construction, build a staff, and launch a state-of the-art hospital from the ground up.

Nelson was a kind, thoughtful, wise leader—and a team player. He took the responsibility seriously because the Kettering Hospital was not just a multimillion dollar business venture. It was a ministry to the community, an extension of the hands of Jesus into one of America's premier cities.

As he brought his group of trusted co-leaders together to pray, they bonded as close friends with a common purpose and with faith that their God would see them over or through or around every mountain, even the big ones. God never disappointed them. Dr. Vernon became a regular prayer partner and the two men, often with others, prayed regularly as the list of obstacles grew. They knew that God would supply answers—His answers—and He did.

As long as he lived, Mr. Nelson never forgot his debt to Dr. Vernon for the spiritual strength he drew from him during difficult days. Woodworking was George Nelson's hobby. He was creative and did splendid, intricate work. Obtaining some beautiful native Ohio walnut, he cured it and built four cabinets for grandfather clocks. One was for his son, one for his sister, one for his own home, and one for Dr. Vernon. It is in the Luthas' living room today as a treasured reminder of their friendship and God's goodness.

Dayton

Because of the Kettering family's involvement in research over decades in America, the intent of Eugene Kettering was that the new hospital would be a tribute to his father, one of the great inventors in the nation. Therefore a 100-bed facility was planned whose primary emphasis would be as a setting for medical research.

However, as the planning progressed, the response from the greater Dayton community was not all positive. Dayton needed more acute-care hospital beds and a broader range of medical services. There simply were not enough facilities to care for the hospitalization needs of the area. Op-ed pieces in the Dayton Daily News were strong and persuasive.

George Nelson, the hospital's first president-elect, knew that the issue was a sensitive one and would need to be handled with more than human wisdom. It would not be wise to turn the feelings of the community against the hospital before it even opened, yet the Ketterings had provided the land and were funding the project, and their dream could not be ignored either.

Nelson worked closely with the Ketterings and also sought community input as plans were refined. The Ketterings developed a deep trust in Mr. Nelson's judgment, but the issue was complicated enough that it was going to take more than smooth talking to keep everyone on board.

Early in the development process President Nelson called Paul Reichert, Treasurer, Martha Johnson, Nursing Administration, and Dr. Luthas together to study the matter and to pray for wisdom and understanding. These unofficial but essential prayer sessions occurred again and again over a period of months each time they approached a sensitive situation. The group leaned more and more heavily on the promise that, *"If you need wisdom—if you want to know what God wants you to do—ask Him, and He will gladly tell you. James 1:5, NLT*

"As long as he lived, Mr. Nelson never forgot his debt to Dr. Vernon for the spiritual strength he drew from him during difficult days."

After the decision was made to go forward to meet the needs of the community for a 300-bed acute-care hospital, virtually everyone was satisfied. The Ketterings were pleased and threw their full support into the project as it broke ground and moved ahead.

God moved mountains to provide just what was needed as the group took seriously the invitation: "If you want to know what God wants you to do—ask Him, and He will gladly tell you."

The Deputy

Dr. Luthas had been invited to help conduct a 5-Day Plan to Stop Smoking in Cleveland, Ohio. He and Betty arrived in Cleveland and drove to the theater to make sure that it was set up properly, the projection equipment was in place, and everything was in readiness.

When they were satisfied that they were ready to begin the meetings, they had one last task—to find a motel. They wanted one nearby and found one near to their site. However, for some reason, they didn't feel clear about it, so they kept checking other places. Not finding one they liked, they returned to the first one—just because it was such a handy location and the price was right. As they stood at the counter checking in, a man approached Vernon and said, "Is this your car?" He motioned to their Mercedes parked out front.

"When Eugene knew that he had called Dr. Luthas he felt that he was now ready for surgery, and they proceeded."

The man introduced himself as a deputy sheriff, and explained that this was part of his beat. He said, "You won't recognize your car in the morning—if it's still here." So they went to a safer motel, marveling at God's protection. He sent the right person, to the right place, at the right time, to provide special protection.

Eugene Kettering

Before the Kettering Hospital had been open very long, Eugene Kettering's health began to fail. He had developed lung cancer, emphysema, and other serious health complications.

His first surgery was done at the Kettering Hospital and he recovered well, but Dr. Robert Taylor, the surgeon, explained to Eugene and Virginia that a second surgery would be needed. Because the Kettering family also owned the Sloan-Kettering Cancer Institute in New York, a discussion developed in the Kettering family as to whether the second surgery should be done at Kettering Hospital in Ohio, or in New York. Eugene had complete confidence in the staff at the Ohio facility and wanted them to do the procedure. But his family prevailed and he went to the Sloan-Kettering Cancer Institute in New York City.

Mr. Kettering knew that because of his health issues he was a high risk surgery candidate and asked the anesthesiologist at Sloan-Kettering to get in touch with Dr. Luthas before the surgery. The New York physician who would be responsible for the anesthesia was president of the American Society of Anesthesia, and one of the best qualified specialists in the nation. However, at Eugene's urging he called Dr. Vernon and they discussed the case. When Eugene knew that he had called Dr. Luthas he felt that he was now ready for surgery, and they proceeded. An unusual bond of trust had developed between Mr. Kettering and Dr. Luthas.

Eugene Kettering died during the surgery. He was 65. His widow, Virginia, died in 2003 at the age of 95.

– Chapter 9 –

His Friends Said ...

During Dr. Vernon's half-century of service and since his retirement, scores of letters, phone calls, and other statements of appreciation have come to him from friends, family, colleagues, and others. Here are just a few:

My Tribute to Dr. Vernon Luthas

"When I first came to Ohio to pastor the Centerville Seventh-day Adventist Church, I quickly became involved in projects that celebrated the Adventist presence in education, healthcare, and witnessing Christ's love and grace in this community. I often heard this phrase, 'The Pioneers' in connection with the resources and wisdom had laid the foundation for our schools, hospitals, and churches in the Dayton area.

"I remember a picture taken at the groundbreaking of the expansion of our Spring Valley Academy where a diminutive, Oriental gentleman was gripping the handles of a large plow signifying the official start to the building project. Dr. Vernon Luthas was referred to as one of the Pioneers of God's work in our hometown.

"Vernon would describe this reference to pioneer fame with the well-known words that preceded almost every spoken thought

he had, 'Let me tell you about my Lord.' Indeed, we who are the beneficiaries of a very solid faith community can celebrate not only the wonderful blessings of God's love and purpose, but pioneers like Dr. Luthas who listened to God's call to grow where we are planted for harvests yet to come.

"If there is one advantage every parish pastor needs, it is the unfailing gift of wisdom that usually resides in the souls of their senior elders. Pastors and churches depend on that one or two certain individuals who become advocates and mentors to the ministers and the ministry of the church. If I may, let me tell you about my Lord ... and how He gifted me with the mind and heart and witness of my friend Vernon. In troubled waters or through smooth passages of my ministry, Vernon was always there to encourage, instruct, and advocate for my pastorate and family.

"Most of all, he is a witness for the goodness of our Heavenly Father. He models patience, joyfulness, and accountability to the call of the gospel. 'Higher than the highest human thought can reach is God's ideal for His children. Godliness, God-likeness is the goal to be reached.' Education p. 18

"When a church and a community are blessed with pioneers and elders like Vernon, for every age, then we are blessed in every way. Let me tell you about my Lord, who causes all of our cups to overflow from the loyalty and faithfulness of this great man."
Sincerely,
Rick LaVenture, Chaplain
Kettering Medical Center

Vern & Betty's daughter and her husband, Diane and Dr. David Doucette's daughter Kristi is now a medical student. She has been impacted by her Grandpa's life and wants to be just like him. As you read the letter below, you'll think you're reading something Vern might have written.

Dear Grandma and Grandpa,

"Thank you so much for helping me with my trip to Papua New Guinea. It is one of the best experiences of my life. I made a promise to God that if he got me into medical school I would go wherever He wanted me to go; I would follow the path He wanted me to follow.

"Grandpa, I think I had a conversation with God like you did when you didn't get into medical school. I was driving and talking to God, and crying so hard I had to pull over. I made a promise to God that if He wanted me to be a doctor I would be a doctor for Him.

"About a week later I got a letter asking me to come in for an interview. Since I've gotten in, I have known that everything that has happened in my life has been God's will. It was hard to decide whether or not to go to Papua New Guinea. I prayed about it a lot and felt compelled to go. For some reason I felt like this was where God was wanting me to go—so I had no choice. I went.

"Let me finish by saying that it was an honor to be a part of the medical team there. It was inspiring to see God working through the staff to help their community. The month I spent there showed me a small window into what it means to help others and to serve. I was given a glimpse into how much God loves all His children.

"I want to continue to have faith and go wherever He sends me next. Thank you so much for your support, your prayers, and love."

I love you so much,
Kristi

A student couple Vern and Betty had helped and encouraged wrote:

"How can we ever begin to show our gratitude for all that you have done for us through the years? Once again you have showered on us the kindness and love that characterize your lives. You have long inspired us and we are continually amazed at what two lives can do when they are surrendered to God's will."

From a student at Loma Linda University:

"I am writing to say that in my Religion class here at Loma Linda University, we had to share with the group the person we consider to have had the strongest spiritual impact on our lives. Dr. Luthas, I could honestly say you have had the greatest influence in my life—teaching and preaching to us kids in Sabbath School in Puerto Rico, your hugs and warm smiles. I just thought I should let you know you have had an impact on my life and my decision to become a physician working with God. Thank you—both for your wonderful example and your love and care."

With much love always,
Shelly Perez Chung
P.S. I'm working on going to Africa with a missionary group this summer!

At Vernon's retirement the Kettering Medical Center Administration and staff wanted to recognize some of his achievements and the fact that he had touched so many lives among them for nearly 40 years. They presented him with a plaque which said:

Vernon Luthas, MD

Dr. Luthas, you are a missionary wherever you are. Your love for God and others shows on your face and flows from your heart to everyone you touch. You spent years in mission work. You have given and raised funds to strengthen others. Your medical practice, full of unselfish ministry, blessed patient after patient.

Now, in retirement, you have spent hours coordinating the prayer ministry at both Kettering and Sycamore Hospitals. Prayer Ministry is not new to you. You carried on a prayer ministry in your anesthesia practice and now, instead of one person having prayer with patients before surgery, you have gathered many volunteers that are a part of this ministry.

Stones thrown into water make a ripple that reaches from shore to shore. Your life creates a ripple of loving care that reaches a multitude. Spots of oasis in the desert sport greet grass and trees because of life-giving water. The living water of your prayer ministry encourages and strengthens both patients and their families.

We give you this LIVING WATER AWARD FOR EXCELLENCE with gratitude. You exemplify the mission of our hospital network and we thank you. You improve the quality of life for the people in the communities we serve.

Kettering Medical Center Network

When Vernon and Betty left the Bella Vista Hospital they were presented with this token of appreciation:

TRIBUTE TO
Vernon C. Luthas, MD

Dr. Vernon C. Luthas will always be remembered at Bella Vista Hospital for his ministry of love and dedication – not only to his profession, but also to his fellow doctors and nurses, to his patients and to this institution. Dr. Luthas served for several extended periods (1967 – 1968 and June 6, 1981 – April, 1987) and later on in his life as a relief doctor on many different occasions. He was always devoted to his church, and especially to the young people.

A whole generation knew him for his stories and sermons as the doctor with the black bag." You never knew what he was coming up with or what he had in his bag as an illustration. Many of these young people are now grown-ups and are serving the Lord in various capacities in the church as teachers, doctors, and technicians, all influenced by his living testimony.

Here at Bella Vista, we will always remember and miss Dr. Luthas and Betty for their labors of love. He will also be remembered as a humble, great, man that inspired others to the love of Christ with sweet, soft words, kind actions and disinterested ways of seeing things.

Bella Vista Academy and many parents will remain forever grateful for the economic assistance given by the Luthas' throughout the years.

God bless you and your family!
Your Bella Vista Family

It Pays to Pray

It pays to pray, it pays to call upon His name,

It pays to pray, to see a miracle displayed.

You'll forget the word IMPOSSIBLE,

When you see the Savior's face,

You'll know He will make a way,

It pays to pray.

Prayer is just as big as God is,

Prayer is just as strong as God is strong,

Prayer can reach as far as God can reach,

Don't ever give up, just pray.

Rodney Griffin

Epilogue

As this book is written, Vernon is retired and Betty's life has been ravaged by Alzheimer's disease, but Vern cares lovingly for her, day and night. When he, as a physician, could see the beginning stages of the disease and realized fully what may be ahead, it was a difficult valley.

One night, unable to sleep, Vern slipped out of bed and sat in the chair in their bedroom, again wrestling with God. He had come to trust Him explicitly but he just needed to talk to Him about it, and he knew he would never be alone.

He told the Lord, "You have entrusted me with my dear wife and I will love and care for her as I vowed many years ago, "in sickness and in health, till death do us part," but please, daily give me the strength, the patience, and the kindness so that Your love always comes through.

And God is daily faithful. In a home where there could be frustration, impatience, and unkind words, Vern has maintained peace because of His presence.

Now his life has changed and taken a turn that they would not have expected. He has become a full-time care-giver. He'll tell you, "Alzheimer's has stolen much of the girl I knew I loved as we stood on the porch that night nearly 60 years ago."

Roles have changed. They can't share memories, trips, or important conversations anymore. He does the cooking, the laundry, the cleaning, and with his limited vision even these routine chores are not easy anymore, but Vernon is still depending on the Lord—on a daily, and sometimes moment-by-moment basis to give him everything he needs, and he is not disappointed.

Vernon Luthas learned early on that God's Word was his compass. He knew that the promises are not only true, but are true for him. In this life Vern will never know the lives he has touched, blessed, inspired, encouraged, ennobled. But there is a common thread that runs through all the stories: You can trust the heart of God to deal with your mountain, no matter how big it is.

Family Photos

The Luthas Family 1940

Standing left to right: Carlton, Claudia, Edward & Vernon; sitting: Irma

Betty and Vernon, October 1993

Vernon and Betty, Christmas 1999

The Doucette Family, Thanksgiving 2010

Back row: David, Seth Kendall

Front row: Diane, Allison, Becka & Kristi Kendall

The Luthas Siblings 2004
Vernon, Irma Puckett & Carlton